Brand Empire
Celebrities

Adam Woog

San Diego, CA

About the Author
Adam Woog has written many books for children, young adults, and adults. He is also a preschool teacher. Adam lives in Seattle with his wife. They have one beautiful daughter.

For more information, contact:
ReferencePoint Press, Inc.
PO Box 27779
San Diego, CA 92198
www. ReferencePointPress.com

LIBRARY OF CONGRESS CATALOGING-IN-PUBLICATION DATA

Names: Woog, Adam, 1953- author.
Title: Brand empire celebrities / by Adam Woog.
Description: San Diego, CA : ReferencePoint Press, Inc., 2016. | Series:
   Collective biographies | Includes bibliographical references and index.
Identifiers: LCCN 2016004097 | ISBN 9781601529947 (hardback)
Subjects: LCSH: Actors--United States--Biography. | Celebrities--United
   States--Biography. | Singers--United States--Biography
Classification: LCC PN2285 .W66 2016 | DDC 791.092/273--dc23
LC record available at http://lccn.loc.gov/2016004097

CONTENTS

From Celebrities to Entrepreneurs

Many people admire others who are wealthier, more powerful, or more famous than they are. So it makes sense that people might look to an admired celebrity for guidance on everyday choices: *What kind of soda should I drink? What clothes are stylish? If it's good enough for my favorite musician, why wouldn't it be good enough for me?*

Businesses understand this, leading to the long-standing practice of using celebrity endorsements to sell products. In this traditional model, a company pays a celebrity to say positive things about its product. Sometimes the celebrity simply lends his or her name to the product, such as a "signature" baseball bat with an athlete's name attached or a guitar bearing a musician's name. The essential message is: *This wine is good, this hat looks sharp. Trust me, you will like it.*

Celebrity endorsement works well and is used everywhere. Although there are no exact figures, it has been estimated that as many as one in four advertisements in the United States feature a celebrity. Business journalist Kevin Harrington comments, "No two products are the same, and no two situations are the same, but celebrity endorsements are almost always a powerful boost to a brand."[1]

Into the New Century

In contrast to traditional celebrity endorsements is the more recent phenomenon of celebrity branding. In this case, famous people use their position in the public eye to launch their own lines of merchandise. They are no longer willing to lend out the glow of their famous names to urge consumers to buy someone else's products. They instead want to explore their creative sides—for instance, by designing clothes—and then market those creations. Traditional endorsement deals are still common, but celebrity branding is, to many observers, the wave of the future. Harrington notes, "Celebrity endorsement is the 20th century; branding is the 21st."[2]

"Celebrity endorsement is the 20th century; branding is the 21st."[2]

—Business journalist Kevin Harrington.

One reason for the growth of celebrity branding is the vast influence of the Internet and social media. People can become famous with lightning speed—sometimes for no apparent reason—because of the Internet's reach. And social media networks multiply this phenomenon as fans hunger for news about their favorite stars. With such easy access to massive audiences, it is increasingly simple for a celebrity to turn fame into commerce. Business writer Deborah Sweeney comments, "It almost comes as a given these days that the hottest new stars will within months turn into self-taught entrepreneurs, creating a fragrance or jewelry line or clothing."[3]

Connecting with Fans

Martha Stewart, Mary-Kate and Ashley Olsen, and many other celebrities have in the past used their names and images to do just that. More recently, Gwyneth Paltrow, Beyoncé, Ellen DeGeneres, Kanye West, Reese Witherspoon, and dozens of others

Like many other celebrities, New York City real estate mogul, reality TV star, and 2016 presidential candidate Donald Trump has attached his name to a variety of products, including bottled water (pictured).

have jumped in as well. Even Donald Trump has a line of signature products; fans can visit his website to pick up items like Trump drinking water, neckties, and fragrances.

The people profiled in this book are only six of the many celebrities today who have used the public spotlight to launch careers in business—careers even more lucrative than those that made them famous. Journalist Roberto A. Ferdman comments, "[They] have harnessed their own personal brands into more successful careers than [entertainment] alone could ever have allowed for."[4]

Jay Z and Diddy are hugely successful rappers who oversee sprawling empires selling everything from luxury clothes to alcohol and sports management. Kim Kardashian has parlayed her TV reality show celebrity into a vast retail fortune built on . . . well, on her celebrity. (The business journal *Forbes* comments, "Kim

Kardashian has monetized fame better than any other."[5]) Jessica Simpson, another reality show star, markets herself as someone with a sensible fashion style that her fans can emulate.

Jessica Alba, meanwhile, has built a huge company in a field—natural, nontoxic products for home and family—that is completely unrelated to the acting career that made her famous. And Taylor Swift has proved to be a genius at extending her musical brand by maintaining a heartfelt, intensely personal connection with her loyal fans. Each in his or her own way, these celebrities are exploring the ways in which fame, personality, and commerce intersect.

> "It almost comes as a given these days that the hottest new stars will within months turn into self-taught entrepreneurs."[3]
>
> —Business writer Deborah Sweeney.

CHAPTER 1

Jay Z

Shawn Corey Carter, known to the world as Jay Z, is widely recognized as one of the world's most prominent musician-entrepreneurs. He has demonstrated a powerful knack for combining musical talent with savvy business practices, both connected intimately with his personal life and taste.

Shawn was born on December 4, 1969. He grew up in Marcy Houses, a complex of buildings for low-income families in what was then a tough neighborhood in Brooklyn, New York. Many of Jay's songs have been about this crime- and poverty-ridden environment and about his family's struggles to maintain a home. He recalls, "We were living in a tough situation, but my mother managed; she juggled. Sometimes we'd pay the light bill, sometimes we paid the phone, sometimes the gas went off. [But] we weren't starving—we were eating, we were O.K."[6]

Shawn's mother, Gloria Carter, was a single parent with three other children: Andrea, Eric, and Michelle. Since their brother became famous, they generally have kept a low profile (less so for his mother, who oversees his charitable foundation).

In many ways Shawn was a typical kid. In the hot New York summers, he liked to splash in water spewing from fire hydrants, play basketball, and ride his bicycle. And he liked to read and to watch TV and videos.

But in other ways Shawn had a difficult life. When he was eleven his uncle was fatally stabbed. That same year his father, Adnes, abandoned the family. And he shot his brother in the shoulder when he was twelve. This happened because Shawn thought his brother, who was abusing drugs, had taken one of his rings. Jay later commented, "I thought I'd go to jail forever. . . . It was terrible. I was a boy, a child. I was terrified."[7]

In high school, drawn into his neighborhood's drug culture, Shawn became a dealer. He regrets this, although he admits it taught him valuable business skills, such as negotiating and budgeting, that would later serve his branding empire well. It also made him fearless. Writer Zack O'Malley Greenburg comments, "When you're used to operating under the intense pressure of the streets, where anything could go wrong and your life is on the line, going into a boardroom with a bunch of guys in suits is a lot less intimidating."[8]

> "When you're used to operating under the intense pressure of the streets, where anything could go wrong and your life is on the line, going into a boardroom with a bunch of guys in suits is a lot less intimidating."[8]
>
> —Writer Zack O'Malley Greenburg.

High School

Throughout these difficult years, there was always one bright spot for Shawn: music. He has often remarked that music saved his life by providing an alternative to crime. Brooklyn was one of the New York neighborhoods where hip-hop music developed, and Shawn developed a strong interest in it—so strong that his nickname was Jazzy. (By his teenage years, this had changed to Jay-Z, and in 2013 the rapper dropped the hyphen and became Jay Z or simply Jay.) Young Shawn wrote his own rhymes, and he often woke his siblings up by drumming patterns on the kitchen table. By the time he entered high school, music was a major passion.

Shawn's first high school was Eli Whitney, a vocational school. But in 1986 the city closed Whitney because of its violence and

Jay Z performs at the American Music Awards in 2009. From an early age growing up in Brooklyn, New York, the rapper had an interest in music, which he eventually decided to pursue as a career.

students' poor academic achievement. Shawn was sent to Westinghouse High, where his classmates included future rappers Notorious B.I.G., Busta Rhymes, and DMX. Shawn next transferred to a high school in nearby Trenton, New Jersey, but dropped out before graduating.

From Novice to Superstar

By this time Jay had decided to walk away from dealing and focus on music. He wanted a goal that would provide an escape from crime but could also earn money. He wrote in *Decoded*, his memoir, "When I committed to a career in rap, I wasn't taking a vow of poverty. I saw it as another hustle, one that happened to coincide with my natural talents and the culture I loved. I was an eager hustler and a reluctant artist. But the irony of it is that to make the hustle work, really work, over the long term, you have to be a true artist too."[9]

It was slow going, but Jay stubbornly persisted. He performed wherever he could, and his first recordings were appearances on albums by two established rappers, Jaz-O and Big Daddy Kane. In time, Jay began to establish a solo career. But he failed to connect with an established record label, so he and a friend formed Roc-a-Fella Records. Jay's first solo album, *Reasonable Doubt*, came out in 1996. Using his knack for entrepreneurship and self-promotion, Jay sold copies from his car and at his performances.

The album was a modest hit. It reached a respectable number twenty-three on the charts compiled by the music industry magazine *Billboard*. And *Reasonable Doubt*'s success led to a deal with a major label, Def Jam. Jay's next release was 1997's *In My Lifetime, Vol. 1*. It was a smash, debuting at number three on the charts and selling more than 1 million copies.

Becoming a Celebrity

What came later, as his millions of fans know, were celebrity and a sprawling retail empire. There are a number of reasons for this success. One of the most important is artistic: His music connects with a global audience. He is one of the best-selling artists in history, with more than 100 million records sold and thirteen number one albums—an unsurpassed record for a solo artist—as of 2015.

The music on those albums appeals to many segments of the listening audience: from young to old, from mainstream rap fans to those who like more experimental styles. His lyrics are intelligent and thoughtful, and the beats accompanying his rhymes are also innovative. This makes Jay Z's songs ready-made for radio and clubs. And he is a dynamic live performer, able to connect personally with even huge stadium audiences.

In addition to his popularity among fans, Jay has been recognized by the music industry: He has won twenty-one Grammy Awards and dozens of other honors, including three wins in the annual American Music Awards, seven BET Awards from Black Entertainment Television, and a place in *Rolling Stone* magazine's 100 Greatest Artists list.

Businessman

Jay Z's musical success made him wealthy, and he used that wealth to create even more income by launching his brand empire; the business magazine *Forbes* estimated his worth at $550 million as of 2015. Gradually, the business took precedence, and in 2003 he announced he was retiring from music. However, he quickly discovered that he missed performing and recording, and in 2005 he "unretired."

> "This attitude that if you do one thing well you can't do something else well is paralyzing for some people—but not for me. If people think that I only make music, they're underestimating me."[10]
>
> —Jay Z

Resuming his music career did not stop Jay Z from fostering his branding empire, however. He has no problem doing both. The musician told a reporter, "This attitude that if you do one thing well you can't do something else well is paralyzing for some people—but not for me. If people think that I only make music, they're underestimating me. I've been a successful businessman my whole career. I can do more than one thing at one time. I can walk *and* chew gum."[10]

Notably, Jay Z became the president of Def Jam Recordings, making him one of the few African American executives of a major label. Jay has used this position to develop young musicians, including Young Jeezy, Rihanna, and Bobby V. But in 2008 Jay Z left Def Jam and launched his own branded label, Roc Nation.

Roc Nation prominently uses Jay Z's name and image to advertise its many activities and products. These comprise the high-end clothing line Rocawear; music production and distribution; and artist and athlete representation, with a client list featuring singers Rihanna and Alicia Keys and sports figures

A Canny Promoter

Jay Z is widely recognized as a canny promoter of his brand. He feels that his music career is just one aspect of his business, which in turn relies on his own fame: "I'm not a businessman, I'm a business, man!" Marketing professional Bridgette Barnett notes some key aspects of his philosophy:

1. Represent your brand. Jay Z is often seen in public wearing, drinking, or using something he makes, so he is a walking advertisement. Repetition helps consumers remember his brand.

2. Represent your people. Jay Z addresses his advertising to his audience directly. This helps develop a sense of loyalty among his fans.

3. Represent your nation. Once Jay Z established a fan base, he expanded his branding empire, which includes a streaming service that helps the careers of some of the world's biggest stars. This in turn leads to respect from his peers in the music industry.

4. Promote your lifestyle. Jay Z makes sure customers know he personally uses items from his brand empire. The technique sends the message: *This is what I consume, and so should you.*

5. Represent your authenticity. Jay Z emphasizes his underprivileged upbringing to establish his authenticity as someone who has risen from the bottom to the top. His Shawn Carter Foundation, which provides scholarships to underprivileged youth, commits him to helping others do the same. This in turn builds loyalty, admiration, and pride.

Quoted in Bridgette Barnett, "How Jay Z Schooled the World in Business & Marketing," Live Oak Communications, April 21, 2015. http://liveoakcommunications.com.

Robinson Cano and Kevin Durant. Roc Nation even sells cigars (Cohiba Comador) and liquor, including Armand de Brignac, an exclusive champagne brand that retails at about $300 per bottle.

Jay Z also makes frequent product endorsements—that is, lends his famous name to another company's advertising. For example, he endorses the luxury watch company Hublot, which markets a $20,000 timepiece called the Shawn Carter.

Moreover, Jay Z promotes his brand through his website, Life + Times, which is devoted to his personal taste in music, fashion, technology, and sports. Although he does mention products sold by others on his website, the focus is on those connected to his own companies, such as the suits he markets through Rocawear or the musical artists who have signed up with Tidal, his music streaming service.

> "My brands are an extension of me, they're close to me. It's not like running GM, where there's no emotional attachment. . . . My thing is related to who I am as a person."[11]
>
> —Jay Z

This personal connection is important to Jay Z. He has often mentioned that he sells only things that he personally would buy. He states, "My brands are an extension of me, they're close to me. It's not like running GM, where there's no emotional attachment. . . . My thing is related to who I am as a person. The clothes are an extension of me. The music is an extension of me."[11]

Controversy

In the past few years, Jay Z has been criticized on several fronts. For one thing, some observers feel that he is losing his reputation for artistic integrity. Celebrity branding expert Jeetendr Sehdev argues that much of Jay's audience finds him too focused on extending his brand, not his music. Sehdev comments, "As a group . . . consumers place a high premium on buying products from brands they see as being honest and having social goals that go beyond those published in their quarterly earnings reports. [Fans] question the exact nature of Jay Z's role in the artistic process. Does he really write his own songs [or] is he just the face of a money-making empire?"[12]

Not surprisingly, Jay Z has defended his role as a business mogul. He asserts that his brand empire does not affect his artistic integrity. For example, critics have questioned his music streaming service, speculating that it is nothing more than an-

Promoting his high-end clothing line Rocawear, Jay Z appears at New York's Fashion Week. Rocawear is only one of the array of products featured in the musician's branded label, Roc Nation.

other moneymaking venture and dismissing his claim that it is devoted only to supporting the musicians who are part of it. Jay Z told a reporter, "The challenge is to get everyone to respect music again, to recognize its value. Water is free. Music is $6, but no one wants to pay for music. You should drink free water from the tap—it's a beautiful thing. And if you want to hear the most beautiful song, then support the artist."[13]

Family Life

Business and music, of course, are not the only things in Jay Z's life—notably, there was his 2008 marriage to another megastar, singer Beyoncé. Like many celebrity couples, the two are private in some ways but are not above revealing some aspects of the lavish lives that their respective careers let them lead. For example, Beyoncé proudly displayed to reporters her $5 million wedding ring.

Their daughter, Blue Ivy Carter, was born in 2012. Two days later Jay Z released "Glory," a song dedicated to her. The newborn's cries can be heard near the end, making her the youngest person ever to appear on a top single. Jay Z jokes to reporters that his daughter is spoiled, and by any measure this is true. Although her parents insist they want her to have a normal childhood, she lives in uncommon luxury: According to the British newspaper *Daily Mail*, the couple spent more than $20,000 on a baby crib, as well as some $80,000 on a diamond-encrusted Barbie doll as a gift for her first birthday.

Philanthropy

Despite such conspicuous consumption, Jay Z and Beyoncé do not spend all of their fortune on themselves and their child. They are also involved to some degree in philanthropy—that is, charitable giving and fund-raising. For example, Jay Z started the Shawn Carter Foundation, which helps provide college scholarships for students with financial or social disadvantages. And he contributes his time and money to support other causes as well, such as joining fellow rapper-entrepreneur Diddy to donate $1 million to the American Red Cross in the wake of Hurricane Katrina in 2005.

Jay Z remains one of the most innovative celebrity entrepreneurs at work today. He has had great success at merging his private life and taste with his music and his businesses. Bono, the lead singer of the band U2, comments, "Jay Z is a new kind of 21st-century artist where the canvas is not just the 12 notes, the wicked beats, and a rhyming dictionary in his head. It's commerce, it's politics, the fabric of the real as well as the imagined life."[14] In the future the rapper will certainly continue to be a major force in both music and business.

CHAPTER 2

Kim Kardashian

Kim Kardashian, arguably the queen of reality TV, is seen by many as an accidental celebrity—that is, someone who is famous only for being famous. But, as her sprawling retail empire has shown, she is actually a strong, shrewd businesswoman who has been able to build and expand that empire thanks to her fame. Furthermore, she displayed this talent for entrepreneurial enterprise early in life.

Kimberly Noel Kardashian was born on October 21, 1980, and raised in the Beverly Hills neighborhood of Los Angeles, California, in a close-knit, wealthy, and prominent family. The family included Kim's older sister, Kourtney; a younger sister, Khloé; and a younger brother, Rob. Their father, Robert, was a third-generation Armenian American. Before his death in 2003 of cancer, Robert was a high-powered lawyer, famous for representing football legend O.J. Simpson during his 1995 murder trial. Kim's mother, Kris, is of Dutch, English, Irish, and Scottish descent.

Kris and Robert divorced in 1991, and Kris married again, this time to Bruce Jenner, a former Olympic gold medalist. They had two daughters of their own, giving Kim several new siblings: three stepbrothers, a stepsister, and two half-sisters. (Soon after

Kris and Bruce divorced in 2014, Jenner underwent a change and became Caitlyn Jenner.)

As a teenager, Kim attended a Roman Catholic all-girls school, Marymount High. During this period she dated TJ Jackson, a member of the group 3T and a nephew of the iconic singer Michael Jackson. Popular in high school, Kim says that she always had a boyfriend. She has also admitted to having had a secret crush on Leonardo DiCaprio, then a star on the TV show *Growing Pains*.

Kim liked to spend hours on the phone and was obsessed with Tae Bo, a martial arts/fitness program. But she says that she was not a very good student. She recalls, "I was okay with school. My sister Kourtney was extremely smart. I always read a little slower. . . . I was like a B student. I didn't love school."[15]

Early Lessons in Finance

Although Kim grew up in a world of wealth and privilege, in some ways her upbringing was traditional and conservative. The family regularly attended church and also stressed the importance of personal responsibility. For example, Robert Kardashian—true to his profession as a lawyer—made Kim sign a contract when she began driving at sixteen, stating that she had to pay for insurance to cover any damage she caused in an accident and pay the fines for any tickets she received. She recalls, "I was in bumper-to-bumper traffic, and I tapped someone. It was so not a big deal, but I had to pay for it."[16]

To earn money for this and other expenses, Kim held various jobs during and after high school. One was at a music company her father owned. She also worked at a clothing store called Body, which she loved and says was "the coolest clothing store in the [San Fernando] Valley."[17]

But Kim's most successful business projects were entrepreneurial. This success was a forerunner of her far greater success as an adult. For example, she bought shoes on eBay and resold them for a profit. To start this venture, her father lent her money—which she had to repay with interest. Her first success was buying five pairs of designer shoes and selling them for a profit of about $6,000.

Kim also started a business cleaning out the closets of the rich and famous. This venture began with her godmother, Bernadette, who was the wife of boxing legend Sugar Ray Leonard. Kim recalls, "Bernadette's closet was massive and had so much stuff in it. I said to her, 'You really need to clean out your closet.' Well, we spent the whole night doing that."[18]

Kim convinced her godmother to let her sell some clothes on eBay in return for a portion of the profit. The venture was a big success. Word spread, and Kim soon had a thriving busi-

Kim Kardashian and Paris Hilton are shown during a night out together in Los Angeles. Kardashian first began to receive public attention in part due to her close friendship with the heiress.

ness doing the same for other wealthy clients, including musician Kenny G, actor Rob Lowe, model Cindy Crawford, and athlete Serena Williams. She recalls, "I discovered eBay and I loved shopping. I had to be on a budget. I didn't have credit cards. How do I figure out how to make this a business?"[19]

Kim says that these early business experiences taught her the importance of having a strong work ethic. She comments, "We grew up with privilege so we knew our standards were high [and] if we wanted to keep it, we had to work hard."[20]

> "We grew up with privilege so we knew our standards were high [and] if we wanted to keep it, we had to work hard."[20]
>
> —*Kim Kardashian*

Rise to Fame

In 2000, when she was nineteen, Kim's romantic life took a turn: She eloped with an older man, a music producer named Damon Thomas. Her mother accepted the marriage, but her father did not approve. In any case it was a stormy relationship, and the couple divorced in 2003 after Kim alleged Damon had physically and emotionally abused her. While waiting for her divorce to be finalized, Kim began dating another musician, singer Ray J.

Until this period, Kim was not famous, but that began to change due to a notorious sex tape of her and Ray J that was leaked to the public, and to her close friendship with wealthy socialite Paris Hilton. But Kardashian's true vault to stardom came in 2007 with the premiere of the reality show *Keeping Up with the Kardashians.* As its faithful watchers know, the program follows the lives of Kim and her extended family. It quickly became the highest-rated series on cable among its target audience: women aged eighteen to thirty-four.

Business Ventures

Most of the people connected with *Keeping Up* thought it would be light, short-lived entertainment. *Los Angeles Times* reporters Harriet Ryan and Adam Tschorn note, "*Keeping Up With the Kardashians* was conceived as . . . the harmless high jinks of a loving

Good Lessons, Bad Mistakes

Kim Kardashian says that as a teen, she learned about financial responsibility from her father. Notably, Robert Kardashian helped her when she started her own businesses as a teenager. He lent his daughter money—but also insisted that she pay it back with interest. Kardashian says that these lessons were invaluable: "I was fortunate for my parents to teach me about credit and saving and things like that. It's nothing they teach you in school, and I really think that is unfortunate. I think classes on credit, and saving, and balancing a checkbook, which is so simple, should be taught in school because a lot of people don't know much about it."

For the most part, Kardashian adds, these early enterprises were successful, although she admits she made some purchases she came to regret. Specifically, she says that she should have focused on items destined to be classics. She recalls:

> I think [it's good] if you stick with classic pieces and just don't buy something that's really trendy. I've bought really stupid things, like jewelry and stuff that I ended up never wearing. I think sometimes you get excited and people are really good at selling things and you just can get overwhelmed. I think it's really important to . . . just make sure that you don't over indulge all the time.

Quoted in Sally French, "The Richer Kim Kardashian Gets, the More She Does This," MarketWatch, July 2, 2015. www.marketwatch.com.

blended family against a backdrop of wealth and famous connections."[21]

Not even Kardashian thought the show would last. Realizing that she could successfully use her fame to further her entrepreneurial ambitions, she saw the program primarily as a way to advertise the businesses she and her sisters were launching, based on their personal shopping taste. These ventures included a chain of clothing and accessory shops called DASH. Kardashian later told a reporter, "When the opportunity for our TV show came about, I wanted to do it to bring attention to our stores. I was thinking this [program] might not last very long, but . . . it would be great press. I didn't think it would turn into what it turned into."[22]

Capitalizing on the show's success, Kardashian shrewdly branched out with new businesses of her own, all prominently featuring her name. One was ShoeDazzle, a shoe-of-the-month club. Others included jewelry inspired by the family's Armenian heritage, perfumes (Kim Kardashian Fragrance), workout DVDs (*Fit in Your Jeans by Friday*), and—of course—more accessories and clothes. She also lent her name to a number of products manufactured by others, including athletic wear, cupcakes, fast food, candles, lollipops, diet products—even a race car.

In 2014 Kardashian branched out further to become a tech entrepreneur when she introduced a mobile app game, *Kim Kardashian: Hollywood*. In it, Kardashian coaches players on becoming celebrities through strategies such as picking out clothes, going on photo shoots and dates, and attending flashy parties. Not surprisingly, the app has attracted millions of downloads.

Personal Events as Cash Cows

Selfish, a 325-page book of selfie photos Kardashian published in 2015, is another example of her gift for promoting herself as a celebrity and, by extension, for promoting her brand. She has proved in many other ways that she can turn virtually everything in her personal life into profit. A prime example was her 2011 marriage to basketball star Kris Humphries. Their televised wedding preparations and ceremony earned an estimated $13 million in ad revenue—with a healthy slice going to Kardashian. *Wall Street Journal* reporter Elizabeth Currid-Halkett comments, "Even Kardashian's participation in a single event—her wedding—can be a cash cow."[23]

> "Even Kardashian's participation in a single event—her wedding—can be a cash cow."[23]
>
> —Reporter Elizabeth Currid-Halkett.

But the marriage was short-lived: Seventy-two days after the ceremony, Kardashian filed for divorce. Although she and Humphries denied the accusations, it was widely rumored that the entire thing was a publicity and moneymaking stunt. In any case the couple's divorce was finalized in 2013.

In the meantime, Kardashian began dating a longtime friend, rapper Kanye West. The couple became parents when

Kardashian and her husband, Kanye West, attend the MTV Video Music Awards in 2015. Married in 2014, the couple has two children, a girl named North and a boy named Saint.

she gave birth to a daughter, North West, in 2013. Kardashian and West were married in May 2014 in Florence, Italy. About a year later, they traveled to Jerusalem so that their baby, who is nicknamed Nori, could be baptized in the Armenian Apostolic

Church. The couple's second son, a boy named Saint, was born in late 2015.

Being a Role Model

As of 2015 Kardashian had some 33 million Twitter followers and 37 million Instagram followers. The buying public has responded so spectacularly to her and her brand for a number of reasons. For one thing, people who buy her products can vicariously experience a little of her glamour, stardom, and love of expensive things. Kardashian says, "Someone can always relate."[24]

Also, Kardashian appeals to her audience because she presents herself as a woman with the power to get what she wants, combined with excellent business sense and a solid work ethic. Kardashian has stated that she thinks she is a role model for anyone who aspires to build a business. She says, "When I was in my 20s, life was about going out, looking cute and having fun with your friends. But as someone who has built her own empire, isn't that a good example for other young girls to follow?"[25]

To this end, Kardashian has come up with three basic rules. First, she says, be methodical and organized. She comments, "It might be really simple, but if you're not fully organized, it becomes a huge problem." Second, have a strong work ethic: "The reality is people don't want to get up and work. It sounds crazy, but I see it all the time." Third, be enthusiastic: "If you find something you're really passionate about, figure out a way to make that your job. Then you'll be happy. If you aren't doing what you want to do, you'll be frustrated."[26]

> "When I was in my 20s, life was about going out, looking cute and having fun with your friends. But as someone who has built her own empire, isn't that a good example for other young girls to follow?"[25]
>
> —Kim Kardashian

With and Without Family

As Kardashian's business empire has grown, reporters have asked if she thinks of herself as a brand separate from her sisters.

She affirms this is true, although she also believes that the whole family is a brand. She comments, "I think that there's the Kim Kardashian brand and the Kardashian brand. I think they blend together, but I have different qualities or interests that my sisters might not be so into. But no matter what, we're family and super close." She adds that her husband is part of the family now, too: "I love working with [Kanye]. I get super inspired when we're together. It doesn't clash for us."[27]

Still, Kim remains the undisputed star of the Kardashian brand name. In 2015 she was the only one to make *Forbes* magazine's annual Celebrity 100 list, with an estimated income for the year of $52.5 million. As of 2015 she has a personal net worth of some $85 million.

Of course, the road to success has not been entirely smooth. For example, Kim and her family became involved in a prepaid credit card business but dropped the project immediately and apologized after it was revealed that the company was cheating consumers.

Apps and More Apps

Kim Kardashian: Hollywood is a game that lets users virtually go on photo shoots and dates and rub elbows with Hollywood elite. It is only the first of what the celebrity hopes will be many more apps. She comments on the wildly successful app:

> Someone can always relate. People always want to get their mind off of things and have something fun to do because their lives are so hectic. It's a fun game that you can really get addicted to and just lose yourself in for a couple of hours.

> I hope to have a bigger presence in the tech world. I love coming up with different app ideas. . . . I feel like I've partnered with the right team, and now I have the creative outlet to make that happen. I'm happy that people are into it and perceiving it well. I just want to create more apps.

Quoted in Lauren Johnson, "After Conquering Reality TV, Kim Kardashian Is Taking the Mobile World by Storm," *Adweek*, March 1, 2015. www.adweek.com.

Another obstacle in Kardashian's rise has involved personal attacks on her lifestyle. For example, the animal rights organization PETA has harshly criticized her for wearing fur coats. Among other tactics, PETA put up a billboard in Beverly Hills that displayed images of her with baby foxes and the caption, "Kim: These babies miss their mother. Is she on your back?"[28] Despite such criticisms, however, Kardashian has reached the rarified world of celebrity branding—and will no doubt stay there.

CHAPTER 3   Sean "Diddy" Combs

The rapper and entrepreneur called Diddy, who excels at thinking outside of the traditional business box, was born Sean John Combs on November 4, 1969. He and his sister, Keisha, grew up in public housing in Harlem, a neighborhood of New York City, and in Mount Vernon, a nearby suburb. Their mother, Janice, a teacher's assistant, raised them because her husband, Melvin Combs, died when Sean was only three. Melvin, who had been involved in the narcotics trade, was murdered in what was probably a drug-related crime.

Understandably, growing up without a father had a serious impact on young Sean's life. Despite the strong upbringing his mother gave him, Sean keenly felt the loss. In particular, he missed having a powerful father figure. He longed for someone who could talk to him about the problems he was having as a young African American. Sean later recalled, "They say you can't miss something you never had, but that's only a little ways right. There's definitely been times as I've gotten older that I've missed my father—his presence—not being here."[29]

Early Years

Sean was always intensely interested in business, and even as a boy he had a knack for entrepreneurship. He demonstrated his ability to think creatively and work hard to expand his horizons and opportunities. Notably, Sean got his first job at age twelve, as a paperboy, an experience that he says was a precursor to his interest in creative business thinking. He told a reporter, "At the time, I wasn't old enough to work legally, so I made a deal with the paper boys who were leaving for college. I told them to let me deliver their papers and I'd send them half of the money. By the time I was 13, I had six routes."[30]

Sean attended high school at an all-boys Roman Catholic school, Mount Saint Michael Academy, where he was a defensive back for the school's football team. During his senior year the team won a division title. But Sean had broken his leg during practice that summer and never played that season. He comments, "I went from the guy whose name was called every two seconds to one where anyone barely spoke to me again."[31]

> "I made a deal with the paper boys who were leaving for college. I told them to let me deliver their papers and I'd send them half of the money. By the time I was 13, I had six routes."[30]
>
> —Diddy

Growing up, Sean had a variety of nicknames, all variations on the word *puff*. Several stories have been told about the origin of these names. According to one, he would huff and puff when he was angry. Another version is that he used to puff out his chest to make his body seem bigger. Over time his nickname changed from Puff Daddy to P-Diddy to the one he now prefers: Diddy.

After graduation, Diddy attended Howard University, a historically black college in Washington, DC. He majored in business but dropped out after two years. The school later awarded Diddy an honorary doctorate, which he said was a great compliment. He told a reporter, "Leaving school early was tough. I'm the type of person who always wants to finish what I start. It was always something in the back of my head."[32]

Business Beginnings

In college the ambitious young man continued to expand his interest in business, supporting himself in part by producing dance parties. He had always been especially interested in the music business, and after dropping out of Howard, Diddy was hired as an intern at Uptown Records, a prominent hip-hop and rhythm and blues label. The company provided him with room and board and only a small salary. But Diddy remained intensely ambitious, and he was soon promoted to being a talent scout, a position that let him help develop the careers of musicians such as Jodeci and Mary J. Blige.

In 1993 Uptown fired Diddy for reasons that are unclear. Still determined to make his mark in the music business, he decided to found his own label, Bad Boy Records. Among the artists the new label signed in its early years were Biggie Smalls (Notorious B.I.G.) and Craig Mack. Bad Boy has since had a hand in producing singles and albums for many other top artists, including TLC, Usher, Lil' Kim, Mariah Carey, and Boyz II Men.

While running his new record company, Diddy also refined his own musicianship. In 1997 Bad Boy released his first album, *No Way Out*, under the name Puff Daddy. It was a smash hit: The album was certified seven times platinum—that is, 7 million copies were sold. The album also spawned several singles, including "Can't Nobody Hold Me Down," which went to number one and spent a total of twenty-eight weeks on the sales charts.

This dazzling debut has led to a steady string of other albums, including *The Saga Continues . . .* , *Press Play*, *Last Train to Paris*, and *MMM*. In addition to this popularity among fans, the music industry has honored Diddy with two Grammy Awards and two MTV Video Music Awards.

Building an Empire

Diddy's career as a performer made him famous, but he became truly rich through ventures outside the music world. The rapper says that music was always crucial to his life. But he also states that it was a way to get a foothold in commercial projects. In other

Sean Combs, today known as Diddy, arrives at the MTV Movie Awards in 2010. Combs showed a talent for entrepreneurship at a young age, beginning his first job when he was only twelve years old.

words, he has always seen himself as a businessman first and a musician second.

And Diddy has proved to be as successful in business as in music. He was the hip-hop world's top earner in 2015, with an estimated income of $60 million for that year alone. As of 2015, *Forbes* business magazine estimated Diddy's total net worth at $735 million.

Like most savvy financial operators, the musician-entrepreneur has diversified into many areas of business. Diversification— spreading investments in many projects, not just one—ensures

A Controversial Scholarship

Diddy has often been criticized for lavishing most of his money on himself and his family, rather than on worthy causes outside his immediate circle. For example, many commentators severely criticized him for giving his son Justin a superluxurious car and then letting him accept a full scholarship to the University of California–Los Angeles two years later. These critics felt that father and son should have declined the scholarship money, enabling it to go to other, needier students instead.

But Diddy defended himself and his son, asserting that he thought the incident was a good learning experience for Justin. In his opinion, Justin had worked as hard as anyone to earn the scholarship, and he deserved it. Diddy commented, "I wasn't annoyed at all. I kind of welcomed it, because if he's going to be doing what he's doing, if he's going to be in the city of L.A., he has to be able to handle the pressure. So I thought it was a great learning tool for him to be humble, handle it and go out there and prove himself on the field and prove himself at school."

Quoted in *Huffington Post,* "Sean 'Diddy' Combs Responds to Justin Combs' Scholarship Controversy," April 8, 2013. www.huffingtonpost.com.

that if one venture does poorly, the successful ones will compensate. This practice comes naturally for Diddy. He states, "I just think that because of my earlier experiences, watching my mom work four or five jobs at a time, I'm wired like that. I have never been one to put all my eggs into one basket. Music was never going to be enough."[33]

Each of Diddy's many projects reflects one of his fundamental business principles: Give the customers what they want—or what Diddy thinks they should want. Taken as a whole, Diddy's brand empire creates a full range of products designed to provide a total lifestyle, so that customers can feel as if they are replicating aspects of his luxurious lifestyle. In short, he aims to provide everything—from the music someone listens to, to that person's clothes, fragrance, drinking water, TV shows, and choice of vodka. He remarks, "I have always seen my job as providing a product. As I've gotten older, that's shifted to providing a lifestyle. . . . All of that is well thought out. That was my dream."[34]

To this end, the entrepreneur's projects include a wildly successful clothing line, Sean John. This venture originally focused on men's sportswear but has since branched out to include business wear, eyewear, children's clothing, and a wide variety of accessories. And Sean John has invested in the high-end label Zac Posen and purchased the hip hop fashion label Enyce.

More Business Ventures

Diddy also owns a TV network called Revolt. The network, which began broadcasting in 2013, focuses on music videos, live performances, and news about the music world. A movie production company of the same name has helped produce feature films such as *Lawless*, a drama about bootleggers in the Prohibition era; *Dope*, a comedy-drama about an awkward high school student who gets involved in a drug deal; and *Undefeated*, an inspiring documentary about a high school football team in Tennessee.

Other examples of Diddy's involvement in media include a pair of reality TV shows: *Making the Band*, about creating and launching musical artists, and *I Want to Work for Diddy*, which—as the name implies—puts contestants in competition for a job with the business mogul. And he still owns half of Bad Boy Records, the label that made him famous.

Outside of clothing and media projects, the ever-expanding empire built around Diddy's name includes many other companies. One prominent example is the company that makes Cîroc, a high-end vodka. The alcohol was not well known until Diddy came on the scene in 2007. Thanks to his association with the label, its sales skyrocketed; it is now the second-largest high-end vodka brand in the United States—with Diddy taking half of the profits.

Of course, Diddy's name is the primary force driving sales of all his products. But Diddy knows that having a great product is just as important as having a famous branded name behind it. Pointing to examples such as his fragrance 3AM or his high-end vodka label, he comments, "The only way you can be successful

Diddy poses with a bottle of Cîroc, the vodka that he promotes. His association with the brand vaulted it from being virtually unknown to being the second-best selling high-end vodka in the United States.

with your branding is if you have a great product to sell. If people go home and aren't happy, that won't work. Your product has to stand up for itself."[35]

Charity

The entrepreneur says that he wants to be recognized for more than these entrepreneurial success stories. He maintains that he wants to be known for his charitable donations as well. He told a reporter, "One of the things I try to tell people, and tell myself, is that I don't want to be known as the person who made the most money. I want to be known as the person who gave the most money away."[36]

However, he has apparently yet to give away a significant amount of his millions or to support worthy causes in other ways. Journalist Kelli Goff comments, "Diddy has given to charity over the years but it has not been a defining part of his persona the way it has for many of his peers."[37]

There are a few exceptions to this. For example, in 2003 he ran in the New York City Marathon, raising $2 million from sponsors for the city's educational system. (He finished in four hours and eighteen minutes.) He has also supported such causes as AIDS research and Daddy's House, which helps inner-city youth through tutoring, scholarships, life skills classes, and summer camps. And along with Jay Z, he pledged $1 million to help support victims of Hurricane Katrina and donated clothing from his Sean John line to victims.

> "One of the things I try to tell people, and tell myself, is that I don't want to be known as the person who made the most money. I want to be known as the person who gave the most money away."[36]
>
> —Diddy

Private Life

Instead of philanthropy, for the most part Diddy's wealth has gone toward his own lifestyle and that of his family. He clearly enjoys the luxury that his instinct for successful business ventures makes possible. For example, he owns several large estates around the world, although he admits that his heart remains in New York City. He told a reporter, "I love New York, it's always been my home. It has everything—music, fashion, entertainment, impressive buildings, huge parks, street cafes. And it's very international, with people from all over the world. I love the hustle of things."[38]

Other aspects of Diddy's lavish lifestyle include a yacht, luxury cars, and a private jet. And he has also been generous toward his family. For example, Diddy gave his first son, Justin, a

$360,000 Maybach automobile for his sixteenth birthday. Diddy has also been generous with his five other children, as well as his ex-girlfriends. Justin's mother is Diddy's high school girlfriend, Misa Hylton-Brim. He adopted another boy, Quincy, whose mother is Kim Porter, another ex-girlfriend. Together Diddy and Kim had another son, Christian, and twin daughters, D'Lila Star and Jessie James. And Diddy's daughter Chance was born to another ex-girlfriend, Sarah Chapman.

> "Diddy has given to charity over the years but it has not been a defining part of his persona the way it has for many of his peers."[37]
>
> —*Journalist Kelli Goff.*

As of 2015 he has been dating model Cassie Ventura. Despite all of these and other romantic involvements, however, Diddy has remained single. He has stated that he is not interested in marriage, commenting, "I think you have to be ready for it. Someone else's heart is involved, and that's just a lot of responsibility."[39] Diddy is reportedly also wary of having to go to court someday if a marriage should end in divorce—a process that could cost him tens of millions. On the other hand, he has also stated that he would be willing to sign a "love contract" between himself and a partner.

Controlling His Temper

Another aspect of Diddy's personal life reflects what he admits is a short temper. For example, in 1999 he and his then girlfriend, actress-singer Jennifer Lopez, attended a Christmas party at a Manhattan nightclub. Gunfire broke out, and in the ensuing investigation Diddy and another rapper, Shyne, were arrested for weapons violations. Diddy was also charged with bribing his driver to say that he owned Diddy's gun. The rapper was acquitted, but Shyne was convicted and sentenced to ten years in prison.

Another example of Diddy's violent temper was an incident in 2015, when Los Angeles police arrested him for assault with a deadly weapon. Diddy attacked one of the football coaches from Justin's University of California–Los Angeles team with a kettlebell (a heavy weight-lifting aid) after witnessing the coach yell at

A Break in the Music Business

Andre Harrell, the head of Uptown Records, gave Diddy a big break when he hired him at age nineteen. It was a life-changing moment—as it was when Harrell fired the young man, for reasons that remain unclear. Diddy recalls:

> As I walked through the record company, I knew that it was exactly where I wanted to be. It felt like home.
>
> I was like a wonder kid at Uptown. The first record I produced sold two million copies—and I'd only produced it because the producer didn't show up. My talent is definitely a gift. I don't understand where it comes from. I don't play an instrument, and I never went to school for music production, but I know exactly how a song should sound and how to give an artist direction.
>
> Anyway, at Uptown, I sold a huge number of records. I was very passionate, and I didn't understand protocol or workplace politics. So I got fired because there can't be two kings in one castle. I wasn't trying to be disrespectful to Andre, but I was fighting so hard. He wanted to be more diplomatic and to make sure everybody felt involved.
>
> Getting fired was one of the best things that could have happened to me. It taught me that putting out a record is a team effort. It taught me how to motivate people. It taught me not to get caught up in my own hype. I'm glad I learned that at a young age.

Oprah Winfrey, "Oprah Talks to Sean Combs." *O Magazine*, http://www.oprah.com/omagazine/Oprah-Interviews-Sean-Combs-P-Diddy-Puff-Daddy

his son. However, Diddy was not convicted, because the coach chose not to press charges. Diddy has defended his actions as self-defense, and he maintains that he needed to set an example to his son by being strong. The entrepreneur commented, "You have to be able to take a lot. As a Combs, my sons, they have to be able to take a lot, you can't have no soft skin."[40] When it comes to such controversy, Diddy is clearly a man of quick temper and strong opinions. But he is also just as clearly a smart and seasoned businessman with a knack for leveraging his famous name to expand his brands. And Diddy has shown his ability to think creatively about new forms his business empire might take—something that will undoubtedly serve him well in the future.

CHAPTER 4

Jessica Alba

Jessica Marie Alba, who gained fame as a teenage actress and has since branched out to become a giant in the natural products business, was born on April 28, 1981, in Pomona, California, a suburb of Los Angeles. She and her younger brother, Josh, grew up in another nearby suburb, La Verne.

Their parents are Catherine and Mark Alba, a now retired air force officer. Jessica says that her mother was an early role model for her, especially in developing a strong work ethic. Jessica told a reporter with pride, "There was nothing [she] didn't do. She was the manager of a movie theater; she went to cosmetology school; she was a bartender, waitress, and then my manager."[41]

Often Lonely

Mark Alba's career in the military meant that the family moved often and lived in several different parts of the country, including Mississippi and Texas, before settling in La Verne when Jessica was nine. Jessica's childhood was often unsettled. Because of the family's moves, Jessica attended eleven different schools before she turned twelve. Also, even when the family settled in La

Verne, her father was still in the military and often away on duty. Furthermore, Jessica was chronically ill with respiratory (breathing) problems, including asthma and pneumonia. She recalls, "I was really sick when I was a kid. My mom was with me a lot, and it was tough on my family because my mom had to spend a lot of nights in a cot next to my bed in the hospital."[42]

This somewhat unsettled life often caused problems. For instance, at one point Jessica's parents enrolled her in elementary school in Del Rio, Texas. School officials, noting her brown skin and Hispanic name, assumed she was a native Spanish speaker. They put her in a bilingual class when, in fact, Jessica did not speak a word of Spanish. It took a little while for her parents to straighten the situation out.

Another result of her frequent moves and absences was that Jessica had difficulty making friends. Because they did not know her, classmates often made fun of her. She recalls that in middle school in California, a group of popular girls shunned her—until they saw her photos in *Seventeen* magazine, where she was already appearing as a model. After that, she says, the girls wanted to be her friend.

But despite her problems, Jessica did well at school. She graduated two years early, at age sixteen, from Claremont High School, near her home in La Verne. And with the help of her parents, she worked hard to overcome her illnesses and uncertainties. She recalls, "I was on a swim team, and I was chubby and slow and dead last—a full two laps last. I was crying and couldn't breathe. My mom and dad were like, 'You started this, you're going to finish it!' My parents made me stick to stuff, pick myself up."[43]

Early Acting

After graduation, Jessica began seriously pursuing her main interest: acting. The profession had fascinated Jessica from an early age. When she was eleven, she convinced her parents to let her enter a competition in Los Angeles, where she won the grand prize: free acting lessons.

Jessica Alba got her start in show business playing small parts as a child. Her breakout role, however, came later when she was cast in the television series Dark Angel.

Less than a year later, she signed with an agent and soon had several modeling jobs and small roles in film and TV, including the 1994 movie *Camp Nowhere* and two TV series, *The Secret World of Alex Mack* and *Flipper*. The star of the latter was a dolphin, so much of the series was set in the water. When she auditioned for the show, it helped that thanks to her mother, who had been a lifeguard, Jessica was already a swimmer and scuba diver. Jessica also appeared in several television commercials, including ads for Nintendo and JCPenney.

Jessica already had experience in front of a camera by the time she graduated from high school. At that point she traveled to New York City to study at a prestigious school, the Atlantic Theater Company, then returned to Southern California and resumed her career. She made a few more movies, winning more prominent roles in the Drew Barrymore romantic comedy *Never Been Kissed* and the comedy-horror film *Idle Hands*.

Becoming a Star

But success eluded Alba until she was nineteen. That year she was selected out of a pool of twelve hundred applicants to star in a high-profile TV series, *Dark Angel*. The show, a science fiction saga set in the future, told the story of Max Guevara, a genetically enhanced supersoldier. It debuted in 2000 and attracted a devoted audience, although it ran for only two seasons.

Alba's starring role shot her to stardom and led to a number of prominent film roles, notably in *Fantastic Four*, *Fantastic Four: Rise of the Silver Surfer*, and *Valentine's Day*. Along the way she won several honors, including an MTV Movie Award, a Teen Choice Award, and a Golden Globe nomination. Meanwhile, she began regularly turning up on lists of sexiest women, including polls taken by *Playboy*, *Maxim*, and *GQ* magazines.

At least in part, these polls reflect Alba's exceptional looks. Her exotic beauty stems from her ethnic background: Her mother has Danish, Welsh, German, English, and French Canadian ancestry, and her father is of Mexican descent. Furthermore, according to the findings of a television series about the genealogy of well-known people, Alba's ancestry also includes southern European Jewish and Native American roots, along with the heritage of the ancient Mayan civilization of South America.

Searching for Healthy Products

In 2004, during the production of *Fantastic Four*, Alba began dating film producer Cash Warren. The attraction was instant. Alba recalls that after she met Warren, she called her best friend and said she had met a man, felt like she had known him forever, and would know him for the rest of her life. Of their subsequent relationship, Alba comments, "The romantic stuff comes and goes, but it's like, does that person have your back? You have to be a team navigating through wherever life may lead you and I want a friend for that."[44]

The relationship became serious, and a few years later Alba became pregnant with their first child. The actress was delighted at the prospect of parenthood. She told a reporter at the time, "I come from a huge family and I'm the oldest of 15 cousins, so I've known I wanted kids. I'm ready to be a mom, and it's a really happy time for us and our families."[45] Warren and Alba's first daughter, Honor Marie Warren, was born in 2008, and the couple got married that same year. In 2011 another daughter, Haven Garner Warren, joined the family. While pregnant with Honor, Alba began a quest that would soon lead to her start as a business mogul. This occurred when she became concerned about finding healthy products for babies and households.

> "I realized over time that when I eliminated fragrances and toxic chemicals . . . it eliminated my allergies and my reactions. And so that was kind of a breakthrough moment for me."[46]
>
> —Jessica Alba

Alba's concern was sparked by a couple of things. One was her knowledge that getting rid of toxic products earlier in her life had improved her health. She recalls, "I realized over time that when I eliminated fragrances and toxic chemicals . . . it eliminated my allergies and my reactions. And so that was kind of a breakthrough moment for me, in knowing that you can control the environment that you live in and it will affect your health."[46]

This realization was bolstered when a baby detergent that Alba used to prewash clothes gave the future mom a serious rash. Worrying what other products might not be safe, Alba began researching the ingredients of items in her bathroom cabinet, the cupboards, and the rest of her house. She realized that much

No Stereotypes

Jessica Alba is proud of her Latina heritage, but she avoids acting roles that are offered to her simply because she looks Latina. She feels that such roles too often portray stereotyped images of Latina women, and she wants to land parts strictly on her acting abilities. The actress comments, "Everyone wants to categorize you and pigeonhole you. I'm half Latin, but I grew up in the States. . . . And I didn't want to be [cast as] the best friend, or the promiscuous girl, or the maid, because those stereotypes still exist with Latin roles. I wanted to be a leading lady. And I thought that because I have brown skin shouldn't make any difference."

Quoted in Andrew Goldman, "Don't Mess with Jess," *Elle*, January 4, 2008. www.elle.com.

of them had potentially harmful substances like petrochemicals, formaldehydes, and other chemicals.

Alba grew frustrated while trying to find healthier and more eco-friendly alternatives. For one thing, alternatives were expensive. This was not a problem for Alba, but they were often beyond the budget of an ordinary family. Furthermore, the small companies that made healthy products usually specialized in only a few particular items. No single company offered a comprehensive array of eco-friendly, safe, and nontoxic items.

Launching a Company

In the course of her research, Alba met Christopher Gavigan, who had experience running Healthy Child Healthy World, a nonprofit organization that helped parents protect their children from toxic risks. They became friends and began talking about ways to remedy the situation. At some point the two had a brainstorm: *Why not create our own company?* It could supply parents with a one-stop source for effective, affordable products. And there was nothing like it in the marketplace. Business writer Clare O'Connor comments, "Like most great ideas, The Honest Company was inspired by a need that wasn't being filled."[47]

Alba and Gavigan chose a name—the Honest Company—that reflected their philosophy. After creating a business plan, they found investors and brought in two other partners, marketing experts Brian Lee and Sean Kane. The group launched its new project early in 2012, and Alba was confident about the business and her role in it because, she says, she already had experience in developing a pragmatic work ethic. She comments, "I've always been business-minded. I approached Hollywood like a business. I was very calculated. I wanted to be treated like a guy; I wanted to put asses in [theater] seats. I saved my money, invested wisely and marketed myself. I've been building my own personal brand over time."[48]

The Honest Company

Alba's confidence was justified—the company was a phenomenon. In its first year it generated an impressive $10 million in revenue, and by 2015 it hit the stratosphere with $250 million in yearly sales. As of 2015 the company was valued at $1.7 billion and employed about 350 people.

> "I've always been business-minded . . . I saved my money, invested wisely and marketed myself. I've been building my own personal brand over time."[48]
>
> —Jessica Alba

Honest's first product was a line of diapers. The company has since expanded to include some 120 products, ranging from dish soap, kitchen cleansers, and detergent to multivitamins, diaper bags, and nursery furniture. The business was initially only online, but its success has attracted brick-and-mortar stores eager to carry its products; companies ranging from small boutiques to giant retailers like Costco, Whole Foods, and Target now carry Honest products.

Alba owns 15 percent to 20 percent of its stock; combined with her income from films, this gives her an estimated personal worth of about $340 million. Her wealth landed Alba a spot on *Forbes* magazine's 2015 list of richest self-made women. (*Self-made* refers to people who have built their fortunes from scratch, not from inherited money, marriage, or similar connections.)

Set Apart

The other celebrities on the 2015 *Forbes* list were Beyoncé, Judge Judy, Oprah, and Madonna. But there is a significant difference between those four and Alba: Their primary occupation—that is, entertainment—provides most of their income. In contrast, Alba has built her fortune not through acting but through a company in a completely unrelated area.

Furthermore, there are important differences between Alba's brand and those typically overseen by other celebrities. First, Honest products are affordable. Alba was determined to offer

Along with business partner Brian Lee, Alba poses alongside packages of Honest products. Although Alba is a driving force behind the eco-friendly, nontoxic brand, she is rarely shown or mentioned in the company's advertising.

products that ordinary people would want—and could easily buy. So, unlike many other celebrities, she does not try to convince anyone to mimic the rich and famous by buying expensive luxury items. Writer Hilary Milnes comments, "Alba isn't trying to curate [direct] our lives from her cushy celebrity perspective."[49]

Still another aspect of Alba's brand that sets her apart is that she has a relatively low-key presence. Most celebrities trumpet their fame in their products, such as Diddy's Sean John clothing line. This makes the connection between celebrity and product obvious. By contrast, although Honest has clearly benefited from its association with Alba's famous name, she is not an overwhelming presence in the company's advertising or product packaging. In other words, there is no "Jessica Alba" brand of products.

> "Alba isn't trying to curate [direct] our lives from her cushy celebrity perspective."[49]
>
> —Writer Hilary Milnes.

Furthermore, other celebrities typically oversee a wide variety of products and services unrelated to each other. For example, Jay Z's sprawling empire includes everything from representation of athletes and musicians to alcohol, clothes, and a video streaming service. Alba's company, on the other hand, focuses on products with a single, clearly defined purpose.

Philanthropy and Controversy

Not everything has gone smoothly for Honest, and it has come under criticism on several occasions. Notably, in 2015 a lawsuit accused the company of falsely calling its products "all natural" when they actually contained some synthetic ingredients. Furthermore, the lawsuit charged that one of Alba's products, a sunscreen, was not effective in blocking the sun's harmful UV rays. Alba has strongly denied the charges and promised to fix any legitimate problems. She told a reporter, "Our formulations are made with integrity and strict standards of safety, and we label each ingredient that goes into every product—not because we have to, but because it's the right thing to do."[50]

A Hard Worker

Jessica Alba has succeeded in transferring her tough work ethic on-screen to her new role as an entrepreneur. She jokes that she put in eighty-six-hour weeks while filming *Dark Angel*, and now she puts in eighty-six-hour weeks running the Honest Company. But, Alba says, she knows that such dedication is necessary in order to achieve the kind of success she seeks. She comments, "If it was easy, everyone would do it. You have to be a little bit crazy; you have to have gumption and tenacity. A lot of people give up at the first roadblock. But, for entrepreneurs, if there isn't another road, we create it. We break concrete; we throw dynamite; we figure it out."

Quoted in Derek Blasberg, "How Jessica Alba Built a Billion-Dollar Business Empire," *Vanity Fair*, January 2016. www.vanityfair.com.

Whatever the outcome of any controversy, Alba has forged ahead with Honest. Today she is making fewer films, concentrating instead on her family and business. She often passes up acting jobs that would keep her away from home. Meanwhile, she devotes significant time, energy, and money to philanthropic causes.

Among these are amfAR, a foundation for AIDS research; Habitat for Humanity, which sponsors volunteers who build houses for those in need; the National Center for Missing and Exploited Children; and 1Goal, which provides education to children in Africa. Alba is also a strong supporter of gay rights, voter registration, and the movement to get young people involved in the political process. And even before she launched Honest, she was lobbying government officials to improve laws about product safety.

At the same time, Alba is planning to expand the Honest Company. Notably, she hopes to extend her brand beyond the United States. For example, in 2015 Honest opened business in South Korea, and distribution deals in other countries are in the works. Alba comments, "We really want to make a difference in the world and people's health."[51] With luck, she says, that is exactly what she will do.

CHAPTER 5

Jessica Simpson

Jessica Ann Simpson—future celebrity, businesswoman, and self-described all-American girl—was born on July 10, 1980, in Abilene, Texas. Four years later she and her parents, Joe and Tina, welcomed another girl, Ashlee, who now has an entertainment career of her own. The Simpson family moved often before settling in the Dallas suburb of Richardson. The moves were needed because Joe, a Baptist minister, took on duties in a succession of churches.

The Simpson family was deeply religious, and Jessica grew up strongly entrenched in Christian faith. Some of her first memories, she says, are of sitting in church and listening to her father preach. She remembers him as a dynamic, inspiring speaker. And her first experiences singing in public were in church choir.

But as an adolescent she began expanding her horizons, and she displayed an appetite for public performance. A turning point came in 1992, when Jessica was twelve. She auditioned in Dallas for a revival of the iconic TV show *The Mickey Mouse Club*—one of fifty thousand entrants nationwide.

Eager but nervous, Jessica sang the hymn "Amazing Grace" and danced to a 1990s pop song, "Ice Ice Baby." She was one of the semifinalists in Dallas, which earned her a trip to the next round of auditions in Orlando, Florida—but she did not make the final cut. Simpson blames this, at least in part, on stage nerves. She also points to her lack of professional experience, which put her at a disadvantage compared to other girls. She recalls, "I was coming from the church choir. . . . I didn't come with headshots [professional photos]. I didn't do Off Broadway. I wasn't on *Star Search*. I wasn't doing all the things these other kids were doing."[52]

A Start

The experience was a huge disappointment, and Jessica thought seriously about quitting. She recalls, "When I got the letter that said I didn't make it, I just remember that I was giving up and I thought that I was going to die."[53] But the feeling passed, and as Jessica's confidence returned she found another opportunity. A guest speaker at the family's church heard her sing and signed her to his gospel music label. The company failed before she was able to make an album. However, Jessica's grandmother gave her money to record an album on her own, and her father started shopping it around to agents and record companies.

In 1997 the aspiring singer struck gold: An entertainment lawyer got her an audition with Tommy Mottola, then the head of Columbia Records. Not surprisingly, Jessica was incredibly nervous before her audition, especially knowing that Mottola was married to pop diva Mariah Carey. She recalls, "I knew he married Mariah and had probably listened to her sing in the shower. That was very nerve-racking, because Mariah was a voice I always did look up to and I would always try and emulate."[54]

But Mottola thought Jessica had potential. He was looking for someone who could perform in a similar style to then teenaged singers Britney Spears and Christina Aguilera. Mottola, impressed by Jessica's talent and clean-cut image, signed her up. He told a reporter, "She had a great little look and a great attitude, a fresh new face, and something a bit different than Britney and all of them. She could actually sing."[55]

Jessica's debut album, *Sweet Kisses*, was released in 1999, and it was a huge success. Its first single, "I Wanna Love You Forever," reached the top five of the *Billboard* Hot 100 sales chart. The full album, meanwhile, went double platinum in the United States, with many more millions sold overseas. There have since been ups and downs in her music career, but as of 2015 Jessica had sold more than 30 million albums worldwide.

Getting Married

As her music career took off, Jessica's private life hit a major milestone. She had been a popular cheerleader at J.J. Pearce High School, and a number of boys had been interested in her, but she did not seriously date anyone. In fact, her father had earlier given her a purity ring, and she had promised to remain a virgin until marriage. That condition—having a reputation as unapproachable—may have been part of her appeal to potential boyfriends. One classmate, Chris Etchieson, later commented, "I'd say she was notoriously single and that was part of the reason she got so much attention."[56]

That single image changed in 1999 when she met Nick Lachey. Nick, six years older than Jessica, was already a celebrity as the lead singer of the pop group 98 Degrees. They met at a Christmas music-industry event, just as her first album was making a splash, and they soon became an off-and-on couple—mostly on.

In 2002 Nick chartered a sailboat in Hawaii, took Jessica on a sunset cruise, and proposed on the water. Jessica recalls that she was dressed casually. She says, "I was wearing a huge sweatshirt that came down to my knees. If I'd known he was going to propose, I would have at least dressed cute."[57]

Pictured here during a 2004 performance, Jessica Simpson first sang in public as part of a church choir when she was a child. She later signed a record contract, and her debut album was released in 1999.

Simpson said yes, and the couple married in late 2002 at the Riverbend Church in Austin, Texas. Three hundred fifty guests attended, and 98 Degrees performed. Jessica later told a reporter that she had been ready for a long time—after all, she commented, marriage was the expected thing for girls in her home environment. She said, "It was what we all wanted. Go to college, get married, and have babies."[58]

Newlyweds

Soon after the wedding, Lachey and Simpson began working on a new project. Inspired by the popularity of reality programming, Joe Simpson had suggested that the cable company

Getting a Checkbook

When she was sixteen, two years before she released her first album and began dating her soon-to-be ex-husband, Nick Lachey, Jessica Simpson got her own checkbook. But the experience was not a success—she kept overdrawing her bank account and all of her checks bounced. Jessica's mother, Tina, had to take the account away. After she became famous, however, Jessica had enough financial savvy to control her resources rather than relying on others. An early assistant, CaCee Cobb, told a reporter, "She asked the other day for a checkbook, and I looked at her like she was kidding. When I met Jess she didn't know how to do anything for herself, because her parents and then Nick always did everything for her."

Quoted in Whitney McNally, "The Simpson," *W*, April 2006. www.wmagazine.com.

MTV produce a show starring his daughter and her new husband, documenting the ups and downs of a couple learning to live together after only six months of marriage.

With Joe as its executive producer, *Newlyweds: Nick and Jessica* premiered in 2003 and was an immediate hit. At its height, the show attracted more than 4 million viewers every week. MTV advertised it as a reality show, but like other such shows, it was heavily edited to make it as entertaining as possible. Each episode was organized around a classic comedy plot, such as having inexperienced Simpson go camping. To make the show funnier, she was portrayed as not too bright. One classic example: Jessica holds up a can of Chicken of the Sea tuna and tells Nick that she is puzzled. She knows it is fish, but the label says "chicken."

Newlyweds was a success for its three seasons, but the marriage was not. The couple split and their divorce was finalized in 2006. But as the marriage foundered, Simpson's career soared—thanks to the show, she was now famous far beyond the music world.

Business

As it turned out, Simpson's career as a singer and TV star was just a springboard to something even bigger: her business. Several factors helped her make the transition. Notably, she discovered a well of self-reliance that she had not known before. She no longer had a husband to help her make important decisions, and despite the presence of her supportive parents, she knew she had to make her mark as an individual. Simpson has remarked that it took her a long time to adjust to this change, but she was thrilled to discover that she could. She told a reporter, "It's so strange. I'm just proud of allowing myself to think and to act and to be. I never wanted to let anybody down. . . . But then you just have to realize that if you're not happy, you can't make anybody else happy."[59]

Encouraged by her newfound sense of personal freedom, she sought out new opportunities—specifically, in the world of retail. Simpson launched the first of the brands bearing her name in 2006, and the business has exploded. By 2015 her branded products were bringing in some $1 billion in sales, and her estimated personal fortune is $150 million.

Like most branded celebrities, Simpson makes heavy use of her name and image to promote her goods, building on her image as an upbeat woman with an everyday fashion sense. Business writer Russ Gager notes, "From her first appearance in the national consciousness as a singer at age 16, Jessica Simpson has characterized all-American fashion, fun and good taste, [and her] style is characterized by its broad appeal."[60]

> "From her first appearance in the national consciousness as a singer at age 16, Jessica Simpson has characterized all-American fashion, fun and good taste."[60]
>
> —Business writer Russ Gager.

Divided into thirty-odd categories, Simpson's branded products include apparel, footwear, bedroom decor, luggage, and accessories. The most popular is her shoe line, the Jessica Simpson Collection. Among her other lines are casual sports clothing, known as Jessica Simpson the Warm Up, and fragrances such as Jessica Simpson Ten. However, some of her ventures have failed, such as a line of dessert-inspired edible body products with names like Jessica Simpson Deliciously Kissable Hair.

Simpson launched her retail empire with the help of an experienced professional, Vince Camuto, but her family has always been closely involved. Notably, her mother, Tina, has been key, advising Jessica on issues such as color palettes (that is, color schemes that go together). Jessica comments, "It's an incredible experience, creatively. I love to work with my mom."[61]

Inspired by Life

Many aspects of Simpson's commercial ventures are inspired by her private life. For example, when she plans a new product, she thinks about how it might appeal to her own family. She told a reporter, "When I'm in approval or inspiration meetings [with marketing and creative teams], I think of what I want my Nana to wear, and what my [daughter] would look adorable in."[62]

> "I have been every size on the planet, and I understand—I feel like I understand women. I know there's all different kinds, you know. There's life and a whole entire world beyond L.A. and New York."[63]
>
> —Jessica Simpson

And Simpson's well-known involvement as a spokeswoman for the Weight Watchers program is extremely personal—it is a direct reflection of her own equally well-known, lifelong diet problems. The actress-entrepreneur has often stated that most American women have the same worries about weight as she, so they can relate.

In fact, in general Simpson believes that her business has succeeded because she understands women who cannot relate to the glamorous models of TV and magazines. She told a reporter, "I have been every size on the planet, and I understand—I feel like I understand women. I know there's all different kinds, you know. There's life and a whole entire world beyond L.A. and New York. And I do understand the Middle America, and their mindset."[63]

Criticism

Like many celebrities, Simpson has lent some support to philanthropic efforts. For example, she advocates for Operation Smile, which provides surgical treatment for children with facial deformities such as cleft palate. And she has she donates goods such as autographed shoes for charity auctions.

However, some critics complain that Simpson has not made significant donations from her personal fortune. And they say that her efforts so far have been ineffective. For example, she traveled to Kenya on behalf of Operation Smile but reportedly spent most of her ten-day charity trip in a luxury resort, canceling scheduled visits with sick children after claiming illness herself. According to branding experts Carol Cone and Anne Erhard, "Simpson was later slammed by humanitarians when a hotel staff member confirmed that she took in a $1,500 safari during the time she was supposed to have been recovering."[64]

Private Life

Just as such slips in Simpson's public life fuel seemingly endless speculation in the media and among fans, so does her private life. For example, her relationship with her parents has been controversial. (Joe and Tina divorced in 2013.)

Her "dadager," the minister turned show business mogul, has been especially provocative. He has been accused of micromanaging his daughter's career, exerting excessive control over everything from her records and TV appearances to the men she has dated. Furthermore, Joe has notoriously made inappropriate or tasteless comments about his famous daughter. In an often quoted 2004 interview with *GQ* magazine, for example, he discussed his daughter's ample breasts and commented, "Jessica never tries to be sexy. She just is sexy. If you put her in a T-shirt or you put her in a bustier, she's sexy in both. She's got double D's! You can't cover those suckers up!"[65]

Other aspects of Simpson's private life have created similar storms of gossip and speculation. Following her divorce, for instance, she was linked with many other celebrities, including singer John Mayer and actors Dane Cook and Johnny Knoxville. But her longest romance was with Tony Romo, the star quarterback of the Dallas Cowboys, whom she met through her father, a loyal Cowboys supporter. A number of football fans were upset with the couple, blaming Simpson for distracting Romo and causing him to perform poorly on the field.

After she and Romo broke up in 2009, Simpson began seeing another football star, retired tight end Eric Johnson of the San Francisco 49ers and New Orleans Saints. Today they have two children: a daughter, Maxwell Drew Johnson, born in 2012, and a son, Ace Knute Johnson, born in 2013. Jessica and Eric married in 2014 and live in Montecito, California.

By all accounts, despite rumors and gossip to the contrary, the marriage is a solid one, and despite the criticisms Simpson remains firmly at the helm of her business empire. In 2015 she sold about half of her clothing brand to a company called Sequential Brands, but she continues to have a major role in its direction. And she remains confident in her own abilities and business savvy, commenting, "There will always be another opportunity, another door to walk through."[66] What that door will be has yet to be revealed.

CHAPTER 6

Taylor Swift

Taylor Alison Swift was born with a head start on her career in music. For one thing, her mother named her daughter after one of her favorite musicians, singer-songwriter James Taylor. More importantly, her family has always been unusually supportive of her drive to the top.

Taylor was born on December 13, 1989, in Reading, Pennsylvania. She has a younger brother, Austin, who is now an actor. Their father, Scott Swift, was a financial executive, as was their mother, Andrea Finlay Swift, before she chose to leave the workforce and stay at home. The Swifts lived on a large property—a Christmas tree farm—in a well-to-do suburb of Reading. They also had a summer home on the ocean in New Jersey.

Young Taylor attended a Montessori preschool and kindergarten, then a private academy, Wyndcroft. As a girl, Taylor loved riding horses and had a small pony. But from a very early age, music was her true passion. She says that one of her most vivid childhood memories is of listening to and singing along with Disney songs. She also often heard her grandmother, a former professional opera singer, sing at church.

Taylor also showed an interest in performing, and by age nine she was attending a local theater school and appearing in its shows. She also started singing wherever she could. She recalls, "I think I first realized I wanted to . . . be an artist when I was 10. And I started dragging my parents to festivals, and fairs, and karaoke contests."[67]

Falling in Love with Country Music

During this period Taylor absorbed a wide variety of music from pop and rock stars like Britney Spears and Paul McCartney to heavy metal bands like Def Leppard—and, of course, singer-songwriters like James Taylor. But it was country music that captured her, especially that of strong, assertive female singers like Shania Twain, the Dixie Chicks, and Faith Hill. She also loved classic country singers such as Patsy Cline and Dolly Parton.

When she was eleven, Taylor began singing at a weekly country music karaoke contest and kept at it until she won. The prize: being the opening act for Charlie Daniels, a well-known country singer. That same year, she performed the national anthem at a Philadelphia 76ers basketball game. Meanwhile, she was learning guitar and writing her first original songs.

Taylor says that throughout her school years, she was an awkward and unpopular girl, the kind that other girls mocked—they made fun of her frizzy hair, lack of sports skills, and fingers that were constantly bandaged from playing guitar intensively. But music was her salvation during those tough moments. She recalls, "You can imagine how popular that made me: 'Look at her fingers. So weird.' But for the first time in my life, those girls could say anything they wanted about me, because I was just going to go home after school and write a song about it."[68]

From the beginning, Taylor's family was strongly supportive. For example, Andrea Swift regularly took her daughter to New

> "I think I first realized I wanted to . . . be an artist when I was 10. And I started dragging my parents to festivals, and fairs, and karaoke contests."[67]
>
> —Taylor Swift

Taylor Swift performs at New York City's famed Madison Square Garden as part of a 2009 concert tour. From an early age, the singer was interested in performing, an interest that she says began at the age of ten.

York City for voice and acting classes. And before Taylor was even a teenager, Andrea accompanied her to Nashville, Tennessee, the center of the country music industry. But the future star recalls that her parents never pushed her—it was her own love of music that drove her. She says, "If I didn't love this, I would probably not have been able to get this far."[69]

In Nashville, Taylor approached record companies with a demo CD of her singing songs mainly by the Dixie Chicks and other established groups. But she was only one out of countless hopeful singers, and record companies turned her down. Still, Taylor was determined to succeed, and she dreamed about her future. She recalls, "I would think about how lucky I would be if people cared about the words I wrote. I would think about how lucky I would be if, one day, I was walking through a mall and saw a little girl with my face on her T-shirt. I would think that if, one day, anyone lined up to ask me to sign something of theirs, that would be a good day."[70]

Standing Out

Taylor needed to find a way to stand out from the pack, and she saw that the key would be writing her own songs. She wanted to convey the typical teenaged emotions she was going through, stating, "I've only thought about it [songwriting] as a way to help me get through love and loss and sadness and loneliness and growing up."[71]

But Taylor had more than just teenage emotion to work with. She also honed a gift for professional, polished writing. John Rich, a respected Nashville producer and musician, comments, "Taylor earned the respect of the big writers in Nashville. You can hear great pop sensibilities in her writing as well as great storytelling, which is the trademark of old-school country song-crafting."[72]

> "I've only thought about it [songwriting] as a way to help me get through love and loss and sadness and loneliness and growing up."[71]
>
> —Taylor Swift

By age fourteen Taylor realized that she had to move to Nashville to seriously pursue a career. Her family, supportive as ever, went along. Scott transferred to his company's Nashville office, and the entire family moved to nearby Hendersonville.

The effort paid off when Taylor was offered a contract with a large company, RCA Records. But she had doubts that RCA was really committed to her. She recalls, "I didn't want to be somewhere where they were sure that they kind of wanted me maybe."[73] And she chafed at the label's insistence that she record only other people's songs.

Because of her dissatisfaction with RCA, Taylor left the label for a then new company, Big Machine, and in 2006 released her debut album—called simply *Taylor Swift*—made up of songs she had written or cowritten. The first single from it was "Tim McGraw," named for the famous country singer. Written during Taylor's freshman year at Hendersonville High School, it talked about the things she and her boyfriend would share after they graduated and went their separate ways—including their love of Tim McGraw.

Stardom

The single and the album as a whole were moderate hits. But it was her next album, 2008's *Fearless*, that made Swift a star. The album, fueled by more of her strong writing, spent eleven weeks at the top of the country music sales charts and was the best-selling album of 2009 in the United States, with a total of 5.2 million copies sold.

Meanwhile, she was beginning to perform—and not only at karaoke contests as she had as a child. In fact, Swift's increasingly busy touring schedule began to conflict with her education. After her sophomore year at Hendersonville High, she transferred to a private academy that let her study even while away from home.

As her fans know well, Swift's subsequent career, in both country and her later excursions into pop- and rock-influenced music, has been phenomenal. It has resulted in multiple awards, including seven Grammy Awards, an Emmy Award, twenty-two *Billboard* Music Awards, eleven Country Music Association Awards, and eight Academy of Country Music Awards.

Swift's multiple awards, of course, reflect both her musical achievements and her spectacular sales history. As of 2015 she has sold more than 40 million albums and 130 million downloads. In 2015 Swift became the youngest woman ever to be in-

Insulted on National TV

In 2009 Taylor Swift's experience of accepting one of the many honors she has received was marred by a bizarre incident. At the MTV Video Music Awards ceremony, she won the Best Female Video for "You Belong with Me." But during Swift's acceptance speech, rapper Kanye West crashed the stage and interrupted her. He grabbed the microphone and told the stunned audience that singer Beyoncé should have won instead because her video was better.

Shocked, Swift was unable to continue and finish her speech. However, when Beyoncé accepted another award later in the show, she called Swift to the stage to finish her own speech. Afterward, Swift was widely praised for handling West's intrusion with grace. The rapper later apologized to her, both privately and publicly.

cluded on *Forbes* magazine's annual 100 Most Powerful Women list. And, not surprisingly, she is wealthy, with an estimated net worth of some $200 million.

Always About the Music

Much of the reason for Swift's success is her intense focus on finding innovative ways to extend her brand by keeping herself and her music in the spotlight. This was true even before she became a star. Journalist Katie L. Fetting comments, "She didn't wait for her market to come to her; she went to them, whether it was delivering cookies to DJs who spun her records or performing a flash concert in a departure lounge at the JFK Airport."[74]

For Swift, being a strong presence in the retail world was a natural extension of this focus. For example, even before she became a household name, she made ads endorsing l.e.i. jeans and Verizon Wireless. More recently she has endorsed many other companies, including Papa John's Pizza, Walgreens, CoverGirl, Diet Coke, Keds, Subway, and Target.

Along the way, she has also launched a number of her own branded product lines. These include clothing such as T-shirts and blouses; posters from her concert tours; jewelry; accessories such as sunglasses, bags, and guitar pick–shaped pendants; and fragrances including Taylor by Taylor and Wonderstruck. All of these items prominently feature her name and image or a slogan or song title associated with her.

However, overall the number of tangible Taylor Swift products is relatively small when compared to those of many other celebrities, because Swift has always focused most of her attention on one thing: her music. In other words, at heart, Taylor Swift's music and the Taylor Swift brand are one and the same.

Approachability

One big reason why Swift has been so successful in creating her brand and ensuring the loyalty of her fans is her image as an ordinary person. Some celebrities typically project an image that they are somehow unique and superior to others. In turn, they try to convince consumers that using their products will make them feel equally special and privileged.

Swift's approach is in stark contrast. Although she is a megastar, she is viewed as approachable, sincere, and down-to-earth. She works hard to treat people like friends, not just fans, and she tries to be always available to them. Journalist Lori Hill comments about these fans, "They crave real, even in their pop songs. People want to know they are not alone, and the 'we're in this together' underlying message of the Swift brand communicates that."[75]

> "They crave real, even in their pop songs. People want to know they are not alone, and the 'we're in this together' underlying message of the Swift brand communicates that."[75]
>
> —*Journalist Lori Hill.*

Swift takes this personal approach to an unusual degree. She is famous for frequently reaching out to her fans directly, surprising them with presents and attention. Sometimes this attention is directed at individuals, other times at groups. For example, she regularly invites groups of Swifties—her most loyal fans—to one of her houses to preview new albums. These visits include treats such as pizza deliveries and homemade snacks.

She may also surprise individuals with gifts and personal appearances. The gift may be something as simple as a handwrit-

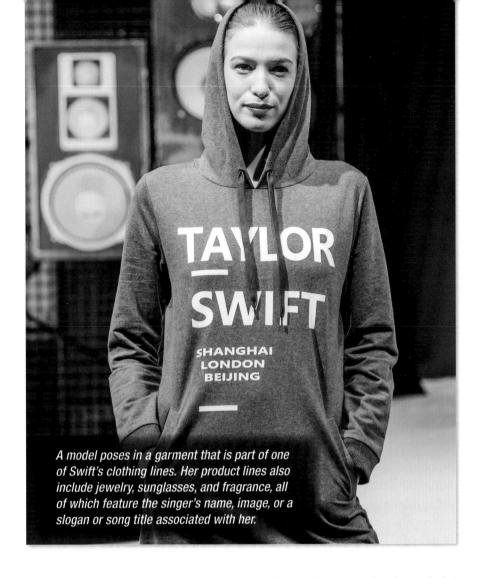

A model poses in a garment that is part of one of Swift's clothing lines. Her product lines also include jewelry, sunglasses, and fragrance, all of which feature the singer's name, image, or a slogan or song title associated with her.

ten note, and sometimes it is more, but it is typically thoughtful and modest. For instance, when Swift heard that one of her fans was going through an especially tough time, she sent the fan a message via Tumblr—and then a care package of clothing, candles, and more. On occasion Swift will unexpectedly show up at a fan's house in person bearing such gifts.

Fighting for Fairness

Swift's commitment to maintaining her brand sometimes extends beyond her fan base and addresses the music industry itself. Notably, she has fought several well-publicized battles to protect her

Publicizing the Importance of Health Checkups

Although in many ways Taylor Swift seems to lead a charmed life, not everything has been upbeat for her. One sobering event was her mother's cancer diagnosis in 2015, which was revealed only after Taylor insisted she have a health checkup. Taylor has since been extremely vocal about encouraging her fans to have regular checkups and urge their loved ones to do the same. On a Tumblr post, she made this point clear: "Your parents may be too busy juggling everything they've got going on to go to the doctor, and maybe you reminding them to get checked for cancer could possibly lead to an early diagnosis and an easier battle. Or peace of mind in knowing that they're healthy and there's nothing to worry about."

Taylor Swift, "Just So You Know…" Tumblr, April 9, 2015. http://taylorswift.tumblr.com.

personal brand from people in the industry who hope to exploit her name and music.

In one of these cases, she is fighting to trademark certain phrases from her songs, such as "This sick beat" and "Party like it's 1989." Business reporter Hugh McIntyre comments that this legal action may seem silly but is actually a wise business decision because it prevents others from marketing Taylor Swift products without her approval. He notes, "Even if she never does make t-shirts and coffee cups with her lyrics on it—each of the dozen-plus trademarks she registered come with certain uses, with categories like 'paper products,' 'musical instruments,' 'handbags' and many more—she certainly doesn't want other companies taking her ideas and turning them into profit."[76]

In two other well-publicized cases, Swift's fight to retain control of her brand and business has shown a broader commitment to protecting all musicians and artists. First, in 2014 she removed her albums from the catalog of the streaming company Spotify. She argued that Spotify's free service, which relies on ads for income, was unfair to songwriters because it denied the musicians a fair share of the profits. Swift was widely praised for the move because she made it clear that all musicians, not just she, were being exploited. Fetting comments, "She framed it expertly, not pleading poverty but emphasizing the worth of music to the world—worth that should be adequately rewarded."[77]

Then in 2015 Swift fought a more public battle with an even bigger music-industry giant: Apple Music. In this case, she passionately objected to Apple's plan to withhold royalties from writers, producers, and artists during its free three-month trial period. In an open letter to the music industry, she stated, "I find it to be shocking, disappointing, and completely unlike this historically progressive and generous company."[78] Once the issue became public, Apple hastily discarded its plans—a measure of how powerful Swift has become in the music industry. Fetting comments, "Can you name another pop star able to smack down a billion dollar multinational like Apple?"[79]

Philanthropy

In addition to her generosity toward fans and her defense of artists' rights, Swift has been unusually active in donating her money and time to various charities—far more so than many other celebrities. She is especially supportive of education, music, and literacy. For example, in a single year she donated $250,000 to schools around the country to buy books, fund educational programs, and help pay teacher salaries. In 2015 she also pledged $50,000 to the Seattle Symphony and $100,000 to the Nashville Symphony, as well as $4 million toward a new education center at Nashville's Country Music Hall of Fame and Museum.

Swift has made many other donations as well, such as six thousand books to the public library in her hometown of Reading, fourteen thousand books to the Nashville Public Library, and all of the proceeds from her song "Welcome to New York" to New York City's public school system.

Swift has also been active in supporting relief efforts for natural disasters. For example, the proceeds from her merchandise sales at the 2008 Country Music Festival went to the Red Cross disaster relief fund, and that same year she sent an additional $100,000 to help the victims of a devastating flood in Iowa. She also donated $500,000 toward relief for victims of Tennessee floods in May 2010. That same year, for a telethon that raised funds for victims of the Haiti earthquake, she performed and answered phone calls from viewers wishing to donate money. And a benefit concert in 2011 raised more than $750,000 for victims of tornadoes.

The singer has also lent her famous voice and face to support a variety of causes she believes in. For example, she has appeared in many public service announcements supporting the Gay, Lesbian & Straight Education Network; a campaign in partnership with the Tennessee Association of Chiefs of Police to protect children from online predators; and an initiative to promote safe teenage driving. She also frequently meets with ill fans in hospitals and through the Make-A-Wish Foundation.

This commitment to philanthropy has earned Swift many honors. Among these was a 2012 Kids' Choice Award presented by Michelle Obama. The First Lady praised her as someone who "has rocketed to the top of the music industry but still keeps her feet on the ground, someone who has shattered every expectation of what a 22-year-old can accomplish, and someone who is going to keep making sparks fly for all of us in the years ahead."[80]

The Sanity Button

Of course, not all of Swift's wealth has gone to charity. Although she lives relatively simply compared to many other celebrities, she owns several homes. Her main residences are two high-rise penthouses, one in New York City and one in Nashville. Swift says she wanted to live in the Nashville apartment building even while it was still under construction. She recalls, "I told my mother, I'm going to live there someday. It just looked so grown-up."[81] Swift also owns homes in Beverly Hills, California, and Watch Hill, Rhode Island. And she bought her parents a lavish home in Belle Meade, a suburb of Nashville.

Like all celebrities, Swift has to balance life in the spotlight with having a private life. Her loyal fans—and even those who are not fans—seem particularly interested in her romantic life. Swift has famously dated a number of men, among them musicians John Mayer, Harry Styles, and Joe Jonas; actors Jake

Gyllenhaal and Taylor Lautner; Conor Kennedy, a member of the famous Kennedy family; and Scottish DJ, musician, and record producer Adam Wiles, who performs as Calvin Harris. The tabloid press has linked her with many others, but as always, such rumors have to be regarded skeptically.

In both her private and professional lives, Swift by all accounts largely succeeds in staying centered and sensible. For instance, she refuses to let herself be caught up in the craziness of fame. She comments, "I have my sanity button that I push. I push this button that's like, 'Stop complaining, your life's great, stop, do not complain about this life, stop, this life is amaaaazing.' Sanity button."[82] It seems likely that the Swift "sanity button" will continue to keep her grounded in the future.

SOURCE NOTES

Introduction: From Celebrities to Entrepreneurs

1. Kevin Harrington, "Celebrity Branding Is Making a Comeback—Tips for Success," *Forbes*, August 18, 2014. www.forbes.com.
2. Harrington, "Celebrity Branding Is Making a Comeback—Tips for Success."
3. Deborah Sweeney, "Kim Kardashian's Most Successful Business Ventures," *Forbes*, November 2, 2011. www.forbes.com.
4. Roberto A. Ferdman, "Music Made Sean 'Diddy' Combs Famous, but Here's What Made Him Rich," *Washington Post*, October 2, 2015. www.washingtonpost.com.
5. *Forbes*, "The World's Highest-Paid Celebrities," June 29, 2015. www.forbes.com.

Chapter 1: Jay Z

6. Quoted in Lisa Robinson, "Jay Z Has the Room," *Vanity Fair*, November 2013. www.vanityfair.com.
7. Quoted in Bill Hutchinson, "Jay-Z Speaks Out About Shooting His Drug-Addict Brother at Age 12 in New Memoir 'Decoded,'" *New York Daily News*, November 22, 2010. www.nydailynews.com.
8. Quoted in Li Zhou, "8 Things Every Entrepreneur Can Learn from Jay-Z," Mic, March 21, 2014. http://mic.com.
9. Quoted in Zhou, "8 Things Every Entrepreneur Can Learn from Jay-Z."
10. Quoted in Robinson, "Jay Z Has the Room."

11. Quoted in Zhou, "8 Things Every Entrepreneur Can Learn from Jay-Z."
12. Quoted in Aaron Taube, "Jay Z's Brand Is Suffering Because People Don't Trust Him Anymore," Business Insider, December 26, 2013. www.businessinsider.com.
13. Quoted in Daily Free Press (Boston University), "Editorial: Tidal Won't Make Waves," March 31, 2015. http://dailyfreepress.com.
14. Quoted in Robinson, "Jay Z Has the Room."

Chapter 2: Kim Kardashian

15. Quoted in Seventeen, "Kim Kardashian Is 17 Again!" www.seventeen.com.
16. Quoted in Aly Weisman, "Kim Kardashian's 3 Rules for Succeeding in Business," Business Insider, May 6, 2015. www.businessinsider.com.
17. Quoted in Seventeen, "Kim Kardashian Is 17 Again!"
18. Quoted in Aly Weisman, "Before She Was Famous, Kim Kardashian Had a Successful eBay Business," Business Insider, May 1, 2015. www.businessinsider.com.
19. Quoted in Ramin Setoodeh, "Kim Kardashian West on Her Empire and Bruce Jenner's Transition," Variety, April 24, 2015. http://variety.com.
20. Quoted in Biography, "Kim Kardashian." www.biography.com.
21. Harriet Ryan and Adam Tschorn, "The Kardashian Phenomenon," Los Angeles Times, February 19, 2010. http://articles.latimes.com.
22. Quoted in Weisman, "Kim Kardashian's 3 Rules for Succeeding in Business."
23. Elizabeth Currid-Halkett, "How Kim Kardashian Turns the Reality Business into an Art," Speakeasy (blog), Wall Street Journal, November 2, 2011. http://blogs.wsj.com.
24. Quoted in Lauren Johnson, "After Conquering Reality TV, Kim Kardashian Is Taking the Mobile World by Storm," Adweek, March 1, 2015. www.adweek.com.
25. Quoted in Setoodeh, "Kim Kardashian West on Her Empire and Bruce Jenner's Transition."
26. Quoted in Weisman, "Kim Kardashian's 3 Rules for Succeeding in Business."
27. Quoted in Setoodeh, "Kim Kardashian West on Her Empire and Bruce Jenner's Transition."
28. Quoted in Emma Akbarein, "Peta Condemns Kim Kardashian's 'Furkini,'" Independent (London), January 21, 2015. www.independent.co.uk.

Chapter 3: Sean "Diddy" Combs

29. Quoted in Zayda Rivera, "Sean (Diddy) Combs Opens Up About Father's Murder for the First Time: He Was a Drug Dealer," *New York Daily News*, October 24, 2013. www.nydailynews.com.
30. Quoted in Ferdman, "Music Made Sean 'Diddy' Combs Famous, but Here's What Made Him Rich."
31. Quoted in Tom Hoffarth, "How 'Undefeated' Brought P. Diddy to Tears—and On Board as Its Exec Producer," *Los Angeles Daily News*, February 16, 2012. www.insidesocal.com.
32. Quoted in Ferdman, "Music Made Sean 'Diddy' Combs Famous, but Here's What Made Him Rich."
33. Quoted in Ferdman, "Music Made Sean 'Diddy' Combs Famous, but Here's What Made Him Rich."
34. Quoted in Ferdman, "Music Made Sean 'Diddy' Combs Famous, but Here's What Made Him Rich."
35. Quoted in Ferdman, "Music Made Sean 'Diddy' Combs Famous, but Here's What Made Him Rich."
36. Quoted in Ferdman, "Music Made Sean 'Diddy' Combs Famous, but Here's What Made Him Rich."
37. Kelli Goff, "What P. Diddy and Mitt Romney Have in Common," *Huffington Post*, June 11, 2012. www.huffingtonpost.com.
38. Quoted in Rosanna Greenstreet, "Q&A," *Guardian* (Manchester), June 20, 2008. www.theguardian.com.
39. Quoted in Francesca Bacardi, "Sean 'Diddy' Combs Would Rather 'Do the Goldie Hawn' than Get Married," EOnline, May 11, 2015. www.eonline.com.
40. Quoted in Naja Rayne, "Sean 'Diddy' Combs on UCLA Incident: 'It Was Just a Miscommunication,'" *People*, August 18, 2015. www.people.com.

Chapter 4: Jessica Alba

41. Quoted in Derek Blasberg, "How Jessica Alba Built a Billion-Dollar Business Empire," *Vanity Fair*, January 2016. www.vanityfair.com.
42. Quoted in Jay Williams, "Jessica Alba Opens Up About Childhood Illness," *ET*, June 4, 2014. www.etonline.com.
43. Quoted in Chelsea White, "'I Was a Chubby Kid!' Jessica Alba Reveals How Her 'Painful' Childhood Pushed Her to Be a Better Mom, Business Woman and Star," *Daily Mail* (London), September 23, 2015. www.dailymail.co.uk.
44. Quoted in Louise Saunders, "Nothing Quite Says 'I Love You' Like a Tweet: Jessica Alba Pays Tribute to Husband Cash Warren with

a Touching Photo Montage as They Celebrate Fifth Anniversary," *Daily Mail* (London), May 20, 2013. www.dailymail.co.uk.

45. Quoted in Andrew Goldman, "Don't Mess with Jess," *Elle*, January 4, 2008. www.elle.com.

46. Quoted in *Huffington Post*, "Jessica Alba on Overcoming Childhood Ailments Through Safe Household Cleaners," April 10, 2012. www .huffingtonpost.com.

47. Quoted in Clare O'Connor, "How Jessica Alba Built a $1 Billion Company, and $200 Million Fortune, Selling Parents Peace of Mind," *Forbes*, May 27, 2015. www.forbes.com.

48. Quoted in White, "'I Was a Chubby Kid!'"

49. Hilary Milnes, "From Gwynnie to Blake: The Brand Bombs of Celebrity Blondes," *Digiday*, July 2, 2015. http://digiday.com.

50. Quoted in Sara Boboltz, "Jessica Alba Slams Accusations Against the Honest Company," *Huffington Post*, September 5, 2015. www .huffingtonpost.com.

51. Quoted in O'Connor, "How Jessica Alba Built a $1 Billion Company, and $200 Million Fortune, Selling Parents Peace of Mind."

Chapter 5: Jessica Simpson

52. Quoted in Rich Cohen, "The Jessica Question," *Vanity Fair*, May 31, 2009. www.vanityfair.com.

53. Quoted in Cohen, "The Jessica Question."

54. Quoted in Cohen, "The Jessica Question."

55. Quoted in Cohen, "The Jessica Question."

56. Quoted in James Robertson, "Jessica Simpson's High School Sweetheart Shares Never-Before-Seen Photos of the Star . . . and Reveals She Was Bullied by 'Jealous Girls,'" *Daily Mail* (London), May 28, 2015. www.dailymail.co.uk.

57. Quoted in *People*, "Jessica Simpson." www.people.com.

58. Quoted in Cohen, "The Jessica Question."

59. Quoted in Whitney McNally, "The Simpson," *W*, April 2006. www .wmagazine.com.

60. Russ Gager, "Jessica Simpson," *Retail Merchandiser*, April 16, 2012. www.retail-merchandiser.com.

61. Quoted in Laurie Sandell, "Jessica Simpson: 'I'm in a Great Place in My Life,'" *Glamour*, August 4, 2009. www.glamour.com.

62. Quoted in Clare O'Connor, "Jessica Simpson's $1 Billion Retail Empire: 'I Understand Women,'" *Forbes*, May 15, 2014. www.forbes .com.

63. Quoted in Kim Bhasin, "Fashion Empire," BloombergBusiness, April 6, 2015. www.bloomberg.com.

64. Carol Cone and Anne Erhard, "Cause & Affect: Fame Game," *Contribute*, 2007. www.contributemedia.com.

65. Quoted in Jo Piazza, "Jessica Simpson Finds a Bosom Buddy," CNN, November 5, 2009. http://edition.cnn.com.

66. Quoted in Cohen, "The Jessica Question."

Chapter 6: Taylor Swift

67. Taylor Swift, "Quotes!," Taylor Swift, June 6, 2012. http://taylorswift.com.

68. Quoted in Vanessa Grigoriadis, "The Very Pink, Very Perfect Life of Taylor Swift," *Rolling Stone*, March 5, 2009. www.rollingstone.com.

69. Quoted in Gayle Thompson, "26 Years Ago: Taylor Swift Is Born in Reading, Pa.," *The Boot* (blog), December 13, 2015. http://theboot.com.

70. Quoted in Thompson, "26 Years Ago."

71. Quoted in Nancy Jo Sales, "Taylor Swift's Telltale Heart," *Vanity Fair*, March 31, 2013. www.vanityfair.com.

72. Quoted in Grigoriadis, "The Very Pink, Very Perfect Life of Taylor Swift."

73. Quoted in Grigoriadis, "The Very Pink, Very Perfect Life of Taylor Swift."

74. Katie L. Fetting, "Five Marketing Lessons from Taylor Swift, Brand Savant," MarketingProfs, July 1, 2015. www.marketingprofs.com.

75. Lori Hill, "The Personable Brand That Is Taylor Swift," Business 2 Community, August 6, 2015. www.business2community.com.

76. Hugh McIntyre, "Taylor Swift Has Trademarked the Phrase 'This Sick Beat,'" *Forbes*, February 4, 2015. www.forbes.com.

77. Fetting, "Five Marketing Lessons from Taylor Swift, Brand Savant."

78. Quoted in Eddy Cue, "Apple Music to Pay Royalties During Free Trial: 'We Hear You Taylor Swift,'" *Guardian* (Manchester), June 22, 2015. www.theguardian.com.

79. Fetting, "Five Marketing Lessons from Taylor Swift, Brand Savant."

80. Quoted in White House, "Remarks by the First Lady at the Kids Choice Awards," March 31, 2012. www.whitehouse.gov.

81. Quoted in Sales, "Taylor Swift's Telltale Heart."

82. Quoted in Sales, "Taylor Swift's Telltale Heart."

FOR FURTHER RESEARCH

Books

Jessica Alba, *The Honest Life: Living Naturally and True to You*. New York: Rodale, 2013.

R.B. Grimm, *Jessica Simpson Unauthorized & Uncensored*. Famous People Collection (Amazon Digital Services), 2015.

Jay-Z, *Decoded*. New York: Spiegel & Grau, 2011.

Jen Jones, *Sean "Diddy" Combs: A Biography of a Music Mogul (African-American Icons)*. Onslow, 2014.

Chas Newkey-Burden, *Taylor Swift: The Whole Story*. New York: Harper-Collins, 2014.

Sean Smith, *Kim Kardashian*. New York: Dey Street, 2015.

Internet Sources

Roberto A. Ferdman, "Music Made Sean 'Diddy' Combs Famous, but Here's What Made Him Rich," *Washington Post*, October 2, 2015. www.washingtonpost.com/news/wonk/wp/2015/10/02/sean-p-diddy -combs-donald-trump-is-not-the-only-person-who-is-a-model-mogul.

Clare O'Connor, "How Jessica Alba Built a $1 Billion Company, and $200 Million Fortune, Selling Parents Peace of Mind," *Forbes*, May 27, 2015. www.forbes.com/sites/clareoconnor/2015/05/27/how-jessica

-alba-built-a-1-billion-company-and-200-million-fortune-selling-parents
-peace-of-mind.

Clare O'Connor, "Jessica Simpson's $1 Billion Retail Empire: 'I Under-stand Women,'" *Forbes*, May 15, 2014. www.forbes.com/sites/clareo connor/2014/05/16/jessica-simpsons-1-billion-retail-empire-i-under stand-women.

Lisa Robinson, "Jay Z Has the Room," *Vanity Fair*, November 2013. www.vanityfair.com/hollywood/2013/11/jay-z-beyonce-blue-ivy-cover -story.

Nancy Jo Sales, "Taylor Swift's Telltale Heart," *Vanity Fair*, March 31, 2013. www.vanityfair.com/hollywood/2013/04/taylor-swift-cover-story.

Aly Weisman, "Kim Kardashian's 3 Rules for Succeeding in Business," Business Insider, May 6, 2015. www.businessinsider.com/kim-kar dashian-how-to-succeed-in-business-2015-5.

Websites

Jessica Alba (www.honest.com/). This is the official site for Alba's business venture, The Honest Company. There are many fansites (as is true with other celebrities), but they sometimes contain inaccurate information.

Sean "Diddy" Combs (http://puffdaddyandthefamily.com). This site is devoted to music, fashion, and other aspects of Puff Daddy's retail lines.

Jessica Simpson (www.jessicasimpson.com). This site focuses on the various brand lines that Simpson sponsors. Among these are her clo-thing, shoes, and fragrance lines.

Kim Kardashian West (www.kimkardashianwest.com). This is the offi-cial site for the reality star, which includes a feature allowing subscribers to get access to live streams and original videos.

Life + Times (http://lifeandtimes.com). A website on which Jay Z de-tails his personal tastes in music, fashion, and more.

Taylor Swift (http://taylorswift.com). The singer's official site includes her frequent blog posts, videos, and more.

INDEX

PICTURE CREDITS